Sorry To Hear About Your Lizard

By: Colleen Hollis

Illustrated and digitized by Colleen Hollis
Copyright © 2024 Colleen's Children Line Inc. Ltd.
Publisher: Colleen's Novels Inc. Ltd.
ISBN: 978-1-964768-26-7

Some look at reptiles and get scared. They just want to run away screaming.

There is truly a special bond between you and your reptile friend. It is a bond that could never be broken.

For us though, it is just like any other pet people might have. Only more cool!

Like having your very own mini dinosaur.

Having a pet has been a big responsibility for you, and you have done a great job.

It's not easy saying goodbye to your pal, and it seems really hard right now.

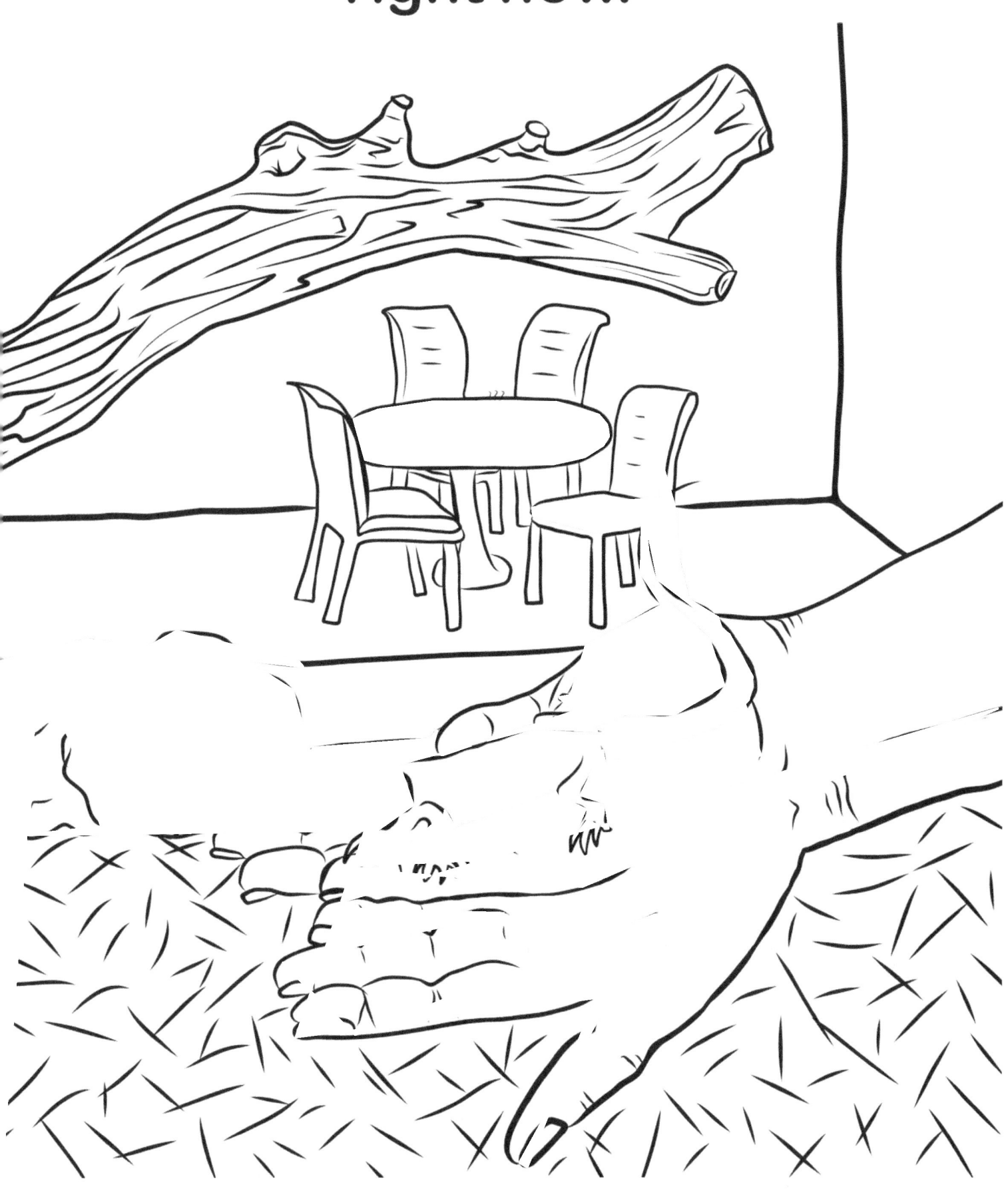

Know in time your frowns will turn into smiles as you reflect fondly back on your scaley friend.

Remember all the fun memories you've made along the way.

Your love for your friend has been a special thing to see.

Even if it feels tough now, you'll
see it will get easier with support.

Or, we can even just sit quietly together if that is what you need.

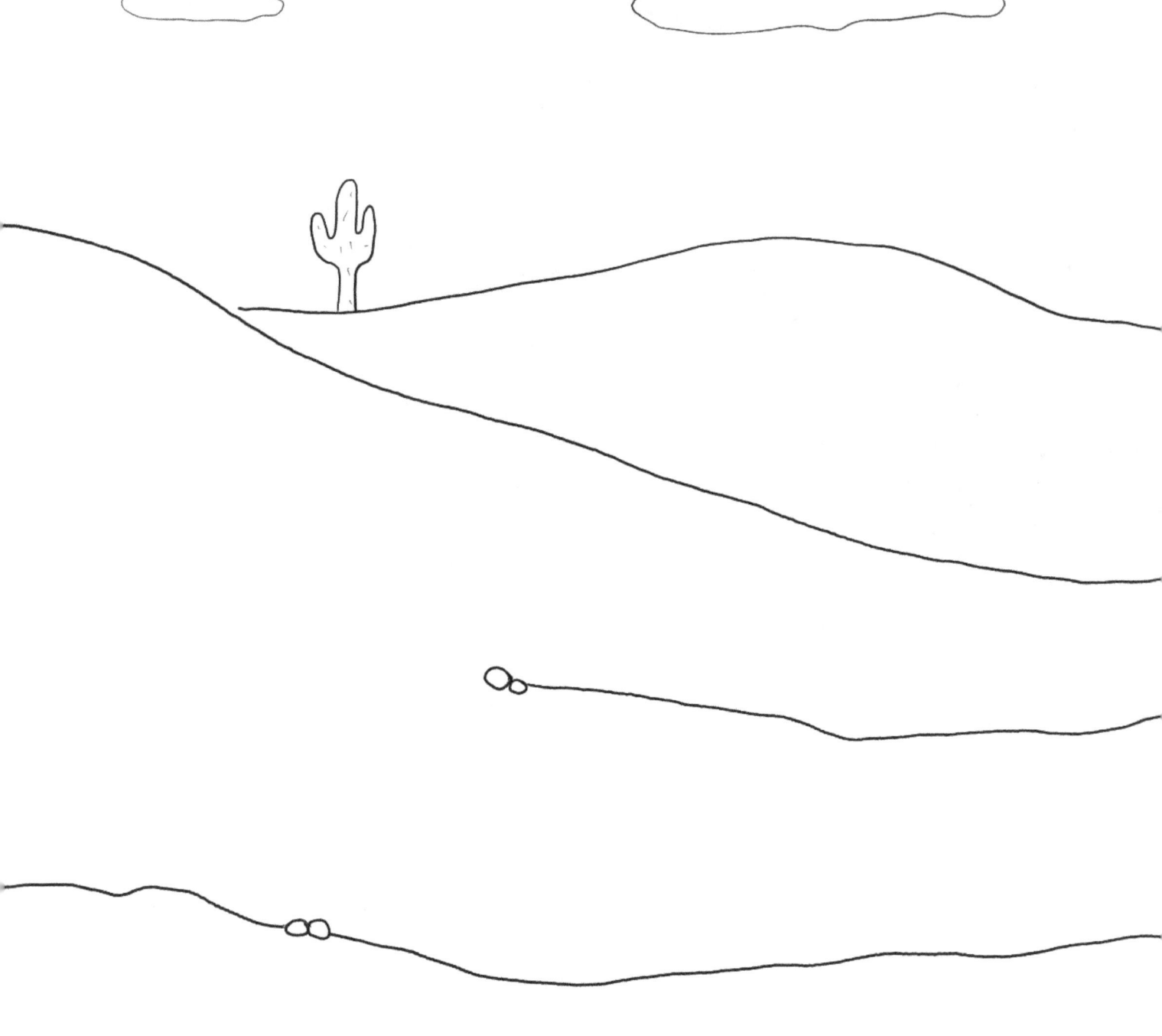

We will get through this together.

Love you forever and always.

Love, _____

Friend's Facts

Friend's Name:_____

Friend's Age:_____

Friend's Favorite Food/s:_____

_____

Friend's Favorite Activity:_____

_____

Friend's Favorite Toy/s: _____

_____

Friend's Favorite Person/s:_____

_____

Feel free to write a little note, or share a memory or two.

Sorry To Hear About Your Lizard, is one of the books in the children's line from Colleen's Bereavement Line For Children. Colleen's Bereavement Line for Children is aimed to assist in the healing process of children that find themselves navigating the loss of a loved one or pet. Sorry To Hear About Your Lizard focuses specifically on those with a reptile friend. A name can be added to the beginning of the book, while in the back of the book there is space to write memories about the scaly friend. Followed by a page for "Friend Facts" that can be filled in for a more personal feel.

All animal books in the series are interactive as well, they are in a coloring book format. Art has been shown as a useful tool that can aid in the healing process.